W0082307

WARD

WARD

Poems

Ryan Vine

Texas Review Press

Huntsville, Texas

Copyright © 2021 Ryan Vine

All Rights Reserved

Printed in the United States of America

Published by Texas Review Press

Huntsville, Texas 77341

Library of Congress Cataloging-in-Publication Data
Names: Vine, Ryan, author.
Title: Ward : poems / Ryan Vine.
Other titles: TRP chapbook series.
Description: Huntsville: Texas Review Press, [2021] | Series: TRP chapbook series
Identifiers: LCCN 2021017009 (print) | LCCN 2021017010 (ebook) |
ISBN 9781680032598 (paperback) | ISBN 9781680032604 (ebook)
Subjects: LCSH: City and town life—United States—Poetry. |
Storytelling—Poetry. | LCGFT: Poetry. | Anecdotes.
Classification: LCC PS3622.I545 W37 2021 (print) |
LCC PS3622.I545 (ebook) | DDC 808.81—dc23
LC record available at https://lccn.loc.gov/2021017009
LC ebook record available at https://lccn.loc.gov/2021017010

Cover and Interior Design: Bradley Alan Ivey

ALSO BY RYAN VINE

Distant Engines

To Keep Him Hidden

CONTENTS

1   Resurrection Ward

2   Short-Order Ward

3   Good Ward Hunting

4   Shavasana Is Not for Sleeping

5   And When His Girlfriend Asks What Took So Long He'll See Himself in the Mirror When He Lies

6   Half Rack Ward

7   Ward Is

8   Water Cooler Cowboy

9   Christmas Party Ward

10   Smartphone Ward

11   The Economist

12   Hot Take

13   Middle Management Ward

14   Orgy Ward

15   Walmart Ward

16   Revision

17   The Dozens

19   Dread Yoga

20   Consultant Ward

21   Party Favor Ward

23   Ward of the Front Porch

24   Quarantine Rex

25   Astronaut Ward

26   To Be Sure

You shall love your crooked neighbor / with your crooked heart.

—W.H. Auden

RESURRECTION WARD

It's simple: I need you,
so you're back

from wherever you were
suffering with all the greats:

Elvis, Biggie, Jesus, Pac.
I've plucked you from your funeral

pyre, laughing at the flames,
rolled with a single word the stone

from time's throat and—voila!—
here you are, wet as a kiss, tough

as tansy, but bruised, I see, I see,
like the legs of a little boy.

We'd tried to step on your dark
head, but like a grub you kept

crawling, shiny and juiced
from the sluicing.

And aren't you lucky, Ward?
No one's here to witness this miracle.

No one even knew you'd disappeared.
You're now allowed to live your lives

like they are one, no questioning
the clinching, no worry about that

sour tug beneath your sappy tone.
Nobody hears it but you

when I open my mouth and caw.

SHORT-ORDER WARD

Don't call it pop.
Please, when

the waitress from the kitchen
surfaces

and the cooks behind her
through their swinging silver door

ache and swoon
try soda

or soft drink.
Call it Coke

even if it's not.
But pop?

Some people
like the waitress

call their fathers that
and even more people

like the waitress
can't stand their fathers

so instead of just watching
her spin, flattening

pleats in her blue dress,
pushing words across

the tiny order pad
you'll have to worry

about what doors
you've sent swinging in her head

and about these tourists
at the counter

who've been staring
since you said it.

GOOD WARD HUNTING

And early in the morning when the men left, high-
stepping through the snowy woods

Ward's girl snuck in and they made one
upper-bunk lump in the hunting shack's backroom.

The two stayed in bed till noon
reapplying Vaseline to their lips, sliding across

each other's faces forward into forever.
Then she had to get going. Work and all.

So when the men dragged their deer back to camp
—threading trails of red snow through the trees—

when they smoked and swore, laughed and spat,
Ward tried to be one of them: a man not afraid

to kill. With each bump of schnapps, each blazing
cig he moved farther and farther away from what

he really wanted: to be in bed, back as one
lump, where he knew he'd found

what he'd spend the rest of his life hunting
but never kill, only wound and keep

wounding.

SHAVASANA IS NOT FOR SLEEPING

Ward's yoga teacher

tells him, delivering

a friendly kick. Dude

has no idea. Poems

are passing through

this darkened room

like neutrinos, man!

The only way to feel

them is just before sleep.

AND WHEN HIS GIRLFRIEND ASKS WHAT TOOK SO LONG HE'LL SEE HIMSELF IN THE MIRROR WHEN HE LIES

Ward's taking a shit
at the Pioneer Bar
sitting in the only stall
with a door, when a man
walks into the bathroom
and says, *you gotta be*
kidding me. Is someone
smoking crack in here?
Ward assumes smoking
crack is a euphemism
for shitting, so he says,
sorry, man. It had to be done.
The man says, *well,*
will you sell me some?
Ward stares for a minute
at his feet and the white
tiles and black squares where
tiles should be then says,
are you fucking with me?
No, man. Sell me some.
I am taking a shit, dude,
Ward says and leans forward
to see if he can see
the man through the crack
between the stall walls,
and there he is, wearing
a faded pink sweater
and looking down into
the sink at his soapy hands,
confused. *Are you telling me,*
Ward says, *that my shit smells*
like crack? The man looks up
into the mirror, surprised
at what he sees there and wipes
his hands on his pants.
Let's pretend this conversation
never happened, he says
and watches himself say,
but before he turns to walk
away, Ward leans back to leave
him there, staring at himself,
standing like a statue in this story.

HALF RACK WARD

The orange construction triangle
is the universal symbol

for Amish.
For bad business decision?

It's mini golf.
You should know these things

because when she's gone
a pile of books will take her place

in bed beside you
and differences like the small ones

between cantaloupe and antelope
will suddenly seem insurmountable.

Multiplication is the rich
man's addition.

The trigger is a spade
with which the soldier digs our graves,

a group of rising water is a wave
and if you really want to know something

about someone, Ward, watch them
drink from a straw.

You'll need to remember this:
nothing makes any sense

if you don't let it.

WARD IS

wise as the resurrected.
Every day

he rises from sleep pierced
and dragging his dreams

like a green blankie behind him.
Today Neilsville, Wisconsin

spreads out as a wake.
Ward's cutting a path through

the swaying barnyard millet,
the darting, sickly barn cats,

to the silo door where the sweet
molasses—you can almost

smell it on him—lifts from piles
of drying feed. Through cubicle aisles

to committees, to the North Shore
Bank he wanders, to Super One

and the DMV, he walks half
in this world arms slightly raised

like he's not walking so much
as he is testing with each step

some fragile, unfamiliar surface
which, Ward, is the surface

that matters, they say, these strange
people to whom these tiny

rooms mean so much.

WATER COOLER COWBOY

Howard says, every morning, "Ward, don't

work too hard." Sometimes

Ward says, "Never do, Howard. Never do."

Sometimes, "Work is all there is, Howard.

Only work." Sometimes Ward says, "Howard,

how about you shut your fucking face

or I swear I'll come back in there

and slap you swollen." Ward says this

as he walks away, of course, under

his breath, more burp than curse.

CHRISTMAS PARTY WARD

If you should walk into a room
and see the woman you love

sharing a bench with another man
leaning over her crossed legs

and into her laugh,
to avoid detection

for god's sake, Ward, don't shuffle.
Just crawl into your pants

hand first through your pockets.

SMARTPHONE WARD

It's like he's out
in his dark backyard
looking for something,

while the dog empties
her bladder before bed,
but the flashlight's

pointed up into his face.
Who cares the city
is throwing its kisses

to the low clouds
so the yard's not
actually dark but

orange, and a helicopter
appears and disappears
somehow soundlessly

it's so far away.
Forget the cars
crossing the harbor's

impossibly large expanse
on the bridge storybook-
high. It doesn't matter

that the dog's chased
a rabbit through a hole
in the fence and her

hackles stand like fins
so she's a big, dumb, hairy
fish barking in the grass.

Through this tiny door
in Ward's hand comes
a kind of anti-light to sink

its straws in and suck. Look,
Ward can see himself. Look,
again, it's Ward! Oooh,

who's that? Ward bets
if he scans the ancient scrolls,
he'll find her last summer

on the riverbank in her
barely-there, sparkly-new
swimming suit.

THE ECONOMIST

Time is our most
precious resource,
he said from the light

of center stage.
So, Ward took his air.
There, we said, you

have two minutes,
maybe three.
Spend it wisely.

HOT TAKE

Ward's all
no thought,
dumb muscle.
It's amazing,
really, how far
he can get.
Puts his head
down, Ward,
and like a drill
through bed-
rock sets in.
Vroom vroom,
through his friends
he pushes past,
vroom! mother,
father, vroom!
brother, sister,
wife, son, daughter,
vroom, vroom,
his job, even
death, vah-
room!, and here
he is, finally,
to the place\
he's always
wanted: pushing
past, frictionless,
inertia-fed,
tumbling
forward into
and through
every god
damn day.

MIDDLE MANAGEMENT WARD

We're going to give you
the go ahead to look into it
like we do our Magic
8 Ball when waiting
for the bubbles to clear.
We want to hear
your take on it, schedule
a sit down to speak,
so to speak, on the topic.
Maybe even give a talk?
We've tried for years
to outsource our crisis
management, but you're
a pro-active player, Ward,
a viable value add. We need
you to drive home a point,
like a toothpick into a plate
of lunchmeat, we mean,
really stick it in there.
So if you wouldn't mind,
if you could just find
a way to go on, like some
decisive action that leads
at some juncture to
confidence in a future
that doesn't involve
self-immolation
etc., etc., that'd be
great. Okay?
Thanks.

ORGY WARD

Ward jumps in
the way

his daddy
taught him to:

feet first.

WALMART WARD

After the girl behind the counter
tells Ward she can't help him, he goes
to the nearly empty shelves himself
to see if he can't solve his own
damn problem. But of course
he can't. He doesn't know
what battery his car needs.
Ward's always thought a battery's
a battery, so now he's back
at the counter asking the woman
to punch some numbers into her robot,
and she tells him, again, she doesn't
know how to look that up. *What about
him,* Ward says, pointing to the man
on the phone. *He's on the phone,* she says.
Right, says Ward and steps back
to wait in line at Walmart. He tries
to be cool, checking his pockets,
counting cracks in the tile, but no,
this is Moloch, he reminds himself,
Moloch, man, Moloch! *We dissolve in the belly,*
he says aloud and heads for the door,
but the motion sensor must be broken,
because he nearly runs into the glass.
He waves his hands at the black eye
and the blue light's blinking, but the door
doesn't move, doesn't make a sound.
The sticker on the glass reads *push
in case of emergency.* Is this
an emergency? Why does every day feel
like an emergency? Others now
have gathered behind him, big men
in denim about to cross the great
parking lot and climb into their
lifted trucks. Is this an emergency?
An old woman shoves a broken walker
across the blacktop. Ward turns back
to the men behind him. The counter
is only a few feet away. The door
opens, and Ward can hear the walker
scraping the linoleum floor, but he
doesn't turn around. A cool breeze
pushes his hair, his collar up.

REVISION

Ward's god.
He takes

the slim pillar
of yesterday

and jumps back
into it, not

as a man
jumping back

into a chute
to endless

happiness,
but as a snake

slithering
into skin

just shed.
Imagine

the straight-
down splitting,

the splintering.
All the new

li(v)es!

THE DOZENS

Your mama got a peg leg with a kickstand.
—Fatlip

Ward's worried about your mom.
Is she ok?

It's just that
when she breathes, it sounds like

we've finally found her
Virginia Slims' missing cellophane,

and Dugan said she's stuck on her stool again
like a gumdrop on a toothpick.

Ward's no doctor, but he plays one
in poems. His official diagnosis

comes mostly from a lifetime of weed-
induced paranoia and a healthy diet

of pharmaceutical commercials.
Maybe it's Asthma? COPD? Itchy

itch syndrome? What about your mom
on her back on the couch and she just can't

reach her afternoon Lucky Charms
(O, the sog!), because the elephant

on her chest refuses to move?
So then Ward asked the doctor

who's paid by Eliquis to recommend
Eliquis what he'd recommend

and Eliquis seems to be the right
treatment for Ward.

But Ward gets ahead of himself.
Do you think your mom could ever

do something like that? Get ahead?
Sorry. What Ward means is

he's not a doctor;
he has only an MFA.

So remember to take everything
he says with a grain of bath salts,

but it sounds like what she has—
your mom—is a bad case of Awake Apnea.

Her breathing is like someone running
her fingers across a thin sheet of ribbed plastic

and suddenly stopping.
Ward should know.

He's successfully diagnosed himself
with a number of ailments:

Adult Deficit Disorder, Tri Bo
years ago. Remember that time

he lanced his own boil?
How about a few questions:

what does she eat? Maybe it's a matter
of how often? Is she depressed?

Does she talk about it? Do you ask?
Has she tried the pill that floats

above the little puffy guy walking down the street?
The one that claims to shade him in the sun

and become umbrella in the rain?
I don't mean to keep prying, really,

but we're trying to get her into the elevator.
Have you suggested she take the stairs?

Maybe a Y membership? That's it:
she could swim. It's obvious

the difficulty she has on land.
In the great, blue pool she could be

like a seal standing in the water,
you know, perpendicular, peaceful,

her long, white whiskers
like the stalled propeller of her face.

DREAD YOGA

Ward's favorite pose? Despair.
It takes some practice

getting there. Like a decade drunk.
You don't just do it on the first day.

Drink hard for a night, sick for two.
Drink hard. Sick. Repeat.

Ten years later look back in wonder.
Another popular pose is trying

to befriend your enemies
to kill them on your side.

Pasty star, you hiss on the floor
and the radiator hisses too and soon

you're floating like you ought to be
back in space, out where no one can see

your weakness. I should have said it
before we began: if you'd like to

set an intention for today's practice
now would be the time.

Because you know what really
salts my salad? Twists my towel?

What absolutely pinches my pickle?
You.

CONSULTANT WARD

Climbing the corporate ladder is simple:
you design a language which confuses

even the experts. The doubt will be
at times so intense, you'll feel

like puking, but it's best to keep talking
though your talking is like sneezing

in the board room with a mouthful of banana.
Down the long table the executives consider

hiring "creatives" and calling this mess "sticky."
Creatives. See what I mean, Ward? The title

which they smile and say is honorific
is really just another way to keep us

in the back room and underpaid.
The conference phone blooms

like a black flower, like an oil slick,
like bubbling tar sands ringing

right through the table.
It's Ward! We've been waiting

for years to pay handsomely
the man who knows

how to disarm a thing after it blows.

PARTY FAVOR WARD

Every time the hostess
laughs her fake laugh

Ward's reminded
of *his* sadness, sees

himself as a boy
waiting at the window.

The food's fine,
and the corner

condo. Part of
the settlement,

Ward guesses:
her Beamer,

this eighth floor
view of Lake Superior's

restlessnesses.
From every room

Ward can watch it,
though he thinks

he spent most of his time
investigating

the reoccurring case
of his missing drink.

Wee! Did you know
it takes four hundred

years for a single drop
of water to make it from

Duluth to the Sault
St. Marie? *You're young,*

she says. *And weird.*
You should spend

time with friends
before they become

their addictions,
their spouses,

their careers.
She stops talking

at last, and leans
across the hallway,

blocking Ward's way
to the bathroom,

as her oily, red wine
slides in circles

in her glass.
What can Ward say?

He whispers your ex
was a fool to leave.

She smiles, nods yes
and kisses the air

as she passes.
On the bathroom ceiling

someone's sloppily
painted over black mold,

thinking it dead.
It threatens,

like a storm cloud,
to spread.

WARD OF THE FRONT PORCH

What bothers you of course,
beyond the smudges on your own window,

isn't so much the yuppies
with their walking poles

walking down the street
but the fact that

they're not even using them.
She just holds hers

both in one hand
and he's sort of dragging

his behind him, leaving
two scratched lines

down the sandy
springtime sidewalk.

Ward, look at the sun
leaning through the windows.

It's time to pour yourself
a bucket of wine

and head outside
where you can criticize

more clearly.

QUARANTINE REX

Ward's mind is still
white hot, but sunk

so far back inside
the cave, that his face

has become a glowing
hole. He stands

like a lamp in the hallway.
Ward is his reading

light at night.

ASTRONAUT WARD

Birth shoots you
into space, and if

you survive the vacuum
of childhood

you're allowed reentry
but only after one

million and one
recalibrations

so what
isn't essential

or at least
what isn't most

Ward

burns away.
And if it doesn't

Ward

burns away
and falls as time

through his mother
and into his child

who both go
crying every night

out the door.

TO BE SURE

Ward, before they click-
close my coffin, please

just push the posers aside
shake me by the shoulders

and give me a good slap
like I wish you would have in life.

ACKNOWLEDGMENTS

Grateful acknowledgment goes to the following journals and newspapers in which these poems, or earlier versions of them, originally appeared:

Minneapolis Star Tribune: "Christmas Party Ward"; *Paper Darts:* "Half Rack Ward."

"Quarantine Rex" & "The Economist" appear in the song cycle "Quarantine Camp" by Raphael Fusco, commissioned by The German Forum of New York and published by Ries & Erler Musikverlag of Berlin.

Thanks to the Arrowhead Regional Arts Council for a 2020 Individual Artist Project Grant. I appreciate your continued support. *The Individual Artist Project Grant is made possible in part by the voters of Minnesota through a grant from the Arrowhead Regional Arts Council, thanks to a legislative appropriation from the arts and cultural heritage fund.*

Thanks to Erik Tschekunow for the love and time he gave to these poems.

Special thanks to Matt Rasmussen and Kathleen Winter for their kind attention.

And a thousand thanks to J. Bruce Fuller and the fine folks at Texas Review Press for bringing Ward back to life.

THE TRP CHAPBOOK SERIES

Series Editor: J. Bruce Fuller

The TRP Chapbook Series highlights work by emerging authors who have not yet released their first full-length book in addition to established authors working on shorter projects.

Books in the series:

Ryan Vine, *Ward*

Richard Boada, *We Find Each Other in the Darkness*

James Jabar, *Whatever Happened to Black Boys?*

Jose Hernandez Diaz, *The Fire Eater*

Kara Krewer, *Born-Again Anything*